TRANSFORMATION
IN
CHRIST

WORKS BY DIETRICH VON HILDEBRAND

IN ENGLISH
In Defense of Purity
Marriage: The Mystery of Faithful Love†
Liturgy and Personality†
Transformation in Christ†
Fundamental Moral Attitudes
Ethics
The New Tower of Babel
Situation Ethics
Graven Images
What is Philosophy?
Not as the World Gives
Man and Woman
The Heart
The Trojan Horse in the City of God
The Devastated Vineyard
Celibacy and the Crisis of Faith
The Encyclical *Humanae Vitae*
Satan at Work

IN GERMAN
Die Idee der sittlichen Handlung
Sittlichkeit und ethische Werterkenntnis
Metaphysik der Gemeinschaft
Das katholische Berufsethos
Engelbert Dollfuss: Ein katholischer Staatsmann
Zeitliches im Lichte des Ewigen
Der Sinn philosophischen Fragens und Erkennens
Die Menschheit am Scheideweg
Mozart, Beethoven, Schubert
Heiligkeit und Tüchtigkeit
Das Wesen der Liebe
Die Dankbarkeit
Ästhetik I & II
Moralia
Der Tod

†*Available from Sophia Institute Press*